BRITAIN AT WAR

COLOUR PHOTOGRAPHS FROM THE SECOND WORLD WAR

CAXTON EDITIONS
AN IMPRINT OF CAXTON PUBLISHING GROUP
20 BLOOMSBURY STREET, LONDON WC1 3QA

© CAXTON EDITIONS, 2002

ISBN 1 84067 293 5

A COPY OF THE CIP DATA IS AVAILABLE FROM THE
BRITISH LIBRARY UPON REQUEST

DESIGNED AND PRODUCED FOR CAXTON EDITIONS
BY KEITH POINTING DESIGN CONSULTANCY

REPROGRAPHICS BY GA GRAPHICS.

ACKNOWLEDGMENTS
THE IMPERIAL WAR MUSEUM

COPY EDITOR
SASHA BEHAR

BRITAIN
AT WAR

COLOUR PHOTOGRAPHS FROM
THE SECOND WORLD WAR

TEXT BY

ANGUS CALDER

CAXTON EDITIONS

A benign side effect of total war was to slow down the process whereby London would be increasingly smothered by motor vehicles and sodium lighting. In the blackout, on nights when there were no raids, the forgotten rays of the moon bathed the city. This undated photograph represents a different time of day from Wordsworth's famous evocation of Westminster Bridge in early morning in 1802:

> This City now doth like a garment wear
>
> The beauty of the morning; silent, bare,
>
> Ships, towers, domes, theatres, and temples lie
>
> Open unto the fields and to the sky;
>
> All bright and glittering in the smokeless air...

But in front of 'Big Ben', that great symbol of empire and democracy, whose clock chimed to announce the nightly war news, there are just two lorries, a cyclist and a tram crossing the great Bridge under a clear sky in which a barrage balloon is just visible. This picture seems to date from 1943.

CONTENTS

INTRODUCTION

THE SECOND WORLD WAR was the biggest enterprise ever entered into by the British State – at this stage, the United Kingdom of Great Britain and Northern Ireland – and the vast overseas Empire which it led or governed. India alone recruited more than two and a half million people to its armed forces. New Zealand, with a population of just 1,630,000, committed a proportion of its national income equal to the UK's contribution to the war, and lost a higher percentage of its population than any other part of the empire. Eire, though until 1948 still nominally part of the British Commonwealth of Nations, declared neutrality. Yet 38,544 people volunteered for the British Armed Forces from Southern Ireland, as well as thousands more Irish citizens living in mainland UK.

It is important to realise that even after the Nazis overran Western Europe in the spring and summer of 1940 and defeated France, Britain's continental ally, the UK never truly 'stood alone'. That said, and even granted the key significance of the Indian Army and Indian war industry, the mainspring of continued resistance to Hitler until the Germans invaded the Soviet Union in June 1941 and the USA entered the war in December, was, and had to be, the effort of the British people.

1n 1939, the ratio of British to German arms production was two to seven. By 1941, this was turned around so that British 'war industry', boosted six-and-a-half times, was out-producing Germany. The basis of this achievement became known as 'war socialism'. Industry, man-power and woman-power were strictly controlled. Nevertheless, Britain's war retained an improvisational, even intimate character. During and after the war, the British were prepared to be convinced by the charming films produced by Ealing Studios that they were a nation of 'little people' able to joke and 'muddle' their way to victory over ruthless, humourless, super-efficient Germans.

Their war went through several distinct phases.

'PHONEY WAR'

It BEGAN ON 3 September, 1939, in doubt and confusion. No one could easily have explained why, after betraying Czechoslovakia to Hitler in the Munich Agreement just under a year before, Britain and France now declared war in support of Poland. The Polish cause in any case was doomed, and within weeks Hitler and Stalin had partitioned the country. So why thereafter did British troops languish in boredom in France behind the supposedly impregnable Maginot Line of forts? In the mid-1930s, Prime Minister Baldwin had memorably declared that 'the bomber will always get through', and apocalyptic plans had been made for an expected German onslaught on London and other cities, from which schoolchildren were evacuated en masse. This famously created stark appositions, as unwashed and verminous urchins, imperfectly toilet trained, from the slums of London, Liverpool and Glasgow were billeted on country gentry with big houses and confronted by such futuristic commodities as carpets and toothbrushes. On the other hand, some town children used to flush toilets, were not impressed when the agricultural labourers who had taken them in advised them to relieve themselves in the fields. Britain resounded with screams of outraged class prejudice.

But there were no huge bombing raids. During the 1930s, principled pacifism had become a considerable factor in British politics, with the Peace Pledge Union attracting large support. The Communist Party, influential among key trade unionists and notable intellectuals, opposed the war now that Stalin was allied with Hitler. Scottish and Welsh national sentiment, not confined to extremists, chafed at fighting 'England's war'. The Ministry of Information, entrusted with propaganda to the home population, was a laughing stock, a by-word for incompetence. Prime Minister Chamberlain, who had given way to Hitler at Munich, had a vast majority in the House of Commons and was a hero for most committed Conservatives, but otherwise lacked charisma.

Meanwhile, citizens blundered around in the nightly blackout designed to deny bombing planes sight of their targets, and young men, called up to the army, tasted the humiliating depersonalisation of service life.

For the navy, there was some interesting action, as when the German battleship *Admiral Graf Spee* was cornered on the River Plate by Uruguay and scuppered by its captain. For pilots in the RAF, who had volunteered for training in peacetime, to be flying at all was a gratification. In 1939, relatively very few people had actually flown, even as passengers. The elderly Chamberlain's gesture in *flying* to Munich was far more dramatic than we can now easily imagine. Cheap airline package tours were two decades away. Boys still in their teens now commanded skies which preserved an aura of virginity and looked down on the patchwork countryside below with the arrogance of those who could see much more than their fellow citizens.

RIGHT: **June 1940. A German soldier displays a captured British tin helmet.**

He holds a standard issue KAR98k rifle and a stick grenade is stuck in his belt. His army has chased the British Expeditionary Force out of France via Dunkirk. It would be strange if the tin helmet was all he had acquired. Looting from enemy corpses and from prisoners was standard practice in all armies. Captured arms and vehicles of course were used. In the North African desert, the opposing armies came eerily to resemble each other, as Hamish Henderson noticed in the third of his *Elegies for the Dead in Cyrenaica:*

> And these, advancing from the direction of Sollum,
> swaddies in tropical kit, lifted in familiar vehicles
> are they mirage – ourselves out of a mirror?
> No, they too, leaving the plateau of Marmarica
> for the serpentine of the pass, they advancing towards us
> along the coast road, are the others, the brothers
> in death's proletariat, they are our victims and betrayers...

BLITZKRIEG

From 8 April 1940, everything except the pilot's 'lonely impulse of delight' changed in a rush of events.

Swedish iron ore was crucial to Germany's war industries. Its only all-weather outlet was the Norwegian port of Narvik. During the winter of 1939-40, the Soviet Union had been fighting Finland. France and the UK had prepared an expeditionary force to seize Narvik under pretence of going to help the Finns. The Germans heard of this and prepared a counter-plan. In mid-March, armistice arrived between Finland and the Soviet Union. The Western Allies turned to a more modest project, laying mines along the Norwegian coast. This was done on 8 April. Next day, the Germans invaded Denmark and Norway. The Royal Navy, which top brass in Britain had confidently thought would deter any such invasion, did indeed maul the German fleet severely but a hastily contrived British expeditionary force manifestly bungled on land. Chamberlain lost his grip on the House of Commons in the famous 'Norway Debate' of 7 May. Numerous Tories voted against the government or abstained. Just before Winston Churchill replaced Chamberlain, news came that the Germans had invaded Belgium and Holland.

During the hectic summer which followed, Churchill's defiant oratory, the resolve of his all-party Coalition Government, and the dedicated efforts of the British news media, rallied public opinion despite a succession of disasters. German *blitzkrieg,* 'lightning war' – fast moving mechanized ground troops supported from the air by planes which included the especially-dreaded *Stuka* divebombers – was more than the surprised French and British could cope with. But the evacuation of most of the British Expeditionary Force from Dunkirk across the Channel over nine days from 26 May to 3 June was represented successfully to the public as a great deliverance, even as a kind of victory, despite the fact that they left behind all their heavy equipment and transport, and despite the loss of 177 precious RAF planes in action over the port. Even the 'Fall of France' – peace was made with Hitler on the 22 June – provoked in many a perverse reaction of relief. King George VI wrote to his mother, 'Personally I feel happier now that we have no allies to be polite to and to pamper'. The newly formed Home Guard of part-time civilians, later remembered as 'Dad's Army', stood pugnaciously ready to struggle against the expected German invasion, though it was very short of serious weapons.

Churchill announced that the Battle of France was over and the Battle of Britain had begun. This term quite soon attached itself to the war in the air between RAF Fighter Command and the Luftwaffe, which was attempting to prepare the way for invasion. Young men flying Spitfires and Hurricanes in sortie after sortie against the German bomber fleet and its protective Messerschmitt fighters were hailed by Churchill and others as knights of the air, timeless heroes. Nevertheless, British losses of planes and pilots and German attacks on airfields had brought Fighter Command very close to destruction when German tactics changed. On 24 August some Luftwaffe planes bombed central London, by mistake, against explicit orders. The British retaliated by bombing Berlin. Hitler now authorised a major assault on London. On 7 September, what the British called their 'Blitz' began. As Fighter Command regained control of the daytime skies, and German invasion plans were called off, London suffered night after night.

Loss of life from bombing in London – 30,000 over the entire war – was small, compared to the tens of thousands who later perished in single nights of Allied raiding against Germany and Japan – at least 35,000 died in one raid on Dresden in 1945. But 'London Can Take It' became a heroic slogan to inspire sympathy all over the world, as civil defence workers toiled heroically to extricate citizens from the ruins of their houses, with US pressmen on hand taking notes. London's noble tenacity also evoked pride, and even jealousy, in every part of the UK. Provincial cities got their chance to emulate it after the Luftwaffe targeted Coventry in a famously destructive raid of 14 November.

In the months that followed, while London continued to receive heavy raids, provincial cities had traumatic 'blitzes'. Liverpool, Birmingham and Plymouth each suffered eight 'major' attacks – 'major' meaning that the Luftwaffe successfully aimed more than 100 tons of bombs at the target. Glasgow-Clydeside had five, Bristol-Avonmouth six. Portsmouth and Southampton were gutted by heavy strikes. Belfast, where defences were scanty, experienced two especially nightmarish raids.

The UK-wide Blitz ended in mid-May 1941, with an especially damaging strike at London. Then Hitler shifted his planes east, planning to attack the Soviet Union. It was also good news that Franklin D. Roosevelt had been re-elected President of the USA and was freer to help Britain, as he wished, with supplies of munitions and foods. Otherwise, news was bad.

Mussolini had brought Italy into the war on Hitler's side in June 1940. An outcome of this was that British troops in Africa (where their prime aim was to secure the Suez Canal and the sea-route to India) scored relatively easy victories against Italians under-equipped for the task of defending Mussolini's African possessions, Libya and Ethiopia. Hitler acted to stiffen his allies. In February 1941, General Erwin Rommel arrived in Africa. Commanding Italians and his own Afrika Korps, he outwitted a succession of British commanders and posed a serious threat to the Canal. In the spring of 1941, German forces swept through Yugoslavia, then Greece, aiming to secure the southern underside of Germany's forthcoming Eastern Front. British forces in Greece were evacuated to Crete. A remarkable German airborne assault by paratroopers captured that island in May 1941. Partial evacuation from Crete, exactly a year after Dunkirk, could not be represented as glorious, and thousands of men were left behind as captives.

Dissatisfaction with British performance in the only arena where Hitler's troops were being fought, conditioned a sour mood regarding, and within, 'war industry', which produced planes, tanks and other munitions. This was further inflamed by news of the valour attributed to Soviet troops after Hitler surprised Stalin by invading through Poland on 22 June. The Red Army, enfeebled by purges of its officers, was at first, in fact, overwhelmed, but 'lightning war' was quenched by the Russian winter and Soviet forces rallied to maintain the cruellest conflict ever seen on earth. British opinion was preponderantly, and often ecstatically, pro-Russian. It seemed a joy to produce tanks to send to this new ally. A completely baseless contrast was readily drawn between the incompetence of the British way of waging war and the supposed majestic virtuosity of Stalin's.

FROM PEARL HARBOUR
TO STALINGRAD

THE JAPANESE air force's surprise strike at the US Fleet in Pearl Harbour, Hawaii, on 7 December was followed by Hitler's declaration of war on the USA, in support of his Far Eastern ally. Barring an all-powerful new German wonderweapon, Britain was now bound to win the war. The resources of the USA were enormous. In 1942, US production of arms would surpass those of Germany, Britain and the USSR combined, and would amount to more than eight times that of Japan. American GIs were soon pouring into Britain in preparation for an assault on Europe. Their ostentatious well-fed prosperity infuriated traditionalists and intoxicated young women. They had smarter uniforms than British soldiers, more pay, and their PX stores were full of such goodies as cigarettes and nylon stockings.

For most of 1942, most Britons did not feel as if the war was sure to be won. Bad news from North Africa persisted. The Japanese swept through the Empire's Far Eastern possessions, and the fall of Singapore on 15 February was a gruesome blow. Soon India itself was threatened. For a time, even Churchill's position seemed vulnerable, as his Coalition began to lose by-elections to independents standing against Conservatives. Rationing of foods deemed essential had been introduced from the outset of war, and was always in itself a popular policy, since it guaranteed fair shares. But its tightening and extension meant that by 1942, diet for most was monotonous. The public might say in polls that it wanted more, not less 'austerity', but in practice the black market thrived. Suddenly, in the autumn of 1942, it was sensed that the tide had turned. Rommel's latest British opponent, Montgomery, prepared carefully for the battle, at El Alamein, from 23 October, which, by 4 November, his men had won. He had nearly twice as many men and more than twice as many tanks. Following his defeat, Rommel fought a gritty retreat, encountering in Tunisia American forces landed in Morocco and Algeria from 8 November.

Meanwhile, where the Don and Volga rivers converged, at Stalingrad, the decisive battle of the European war was taking place. German troops had entered the city on 12 September. They took two thirds of it, but were halted by ferocious Soviet defence. By 23 November, the attackers were themselves encircled, and despite Hitler's continued personal determination that Stalingrad must be taken, his General Paulus at last surrendered on 31 January 1943. The German Army had lost 200,000 men at Stalingrad. From now on, it was in retreat in the East. On 10 July 1943, American and British troops pursued the Germans from Tunisia to Sicily. Fighting up the long Italian peninsula proved hard, but here too, Germans were on the defensive. In the Far East, while Americans reasserted themselves against the Japanese, the turning point in Britain's war came in March 1944, when the Japanese, thrusting into India, were defeated with enormous losses at Imphal.

As Allied bombers pounded German cities, troops were massed in Britain for invasion of Europe. This was launched at last on D-Day, 6 June,1944.

D-DAY TO VJ DAY

About 23,000 allied paratroopers were dropped in Normandy. More than 130,000 troops were conveyed to the 'invasion beaches'. Hundreds of thousands more swiftly followed but progress was exasperatingly slow in the face of solid German resistance over an awkward terrain. Meanwhile, the Germans launched a novel weapon. The first V1 flying bombs were directed towards London on 13 June. These small jet-powered aircraft puttered along at up to 420 mph till they crashed and exploded. While less than one third of nearly 2,500 aimed at London by the end of June actually reached the city, they disrupted daily life as people heard them overhead. They kept coming, though in smaller numbers, till the end of March 1945, eventually causing over 24,000 casualties. The first V2 rocket arrived on 8 September 1944. Flying at a maximum speed of 3,600 mph, rockets at least were not heard before they came to ground. Over seven months, an average of three a day hit London, killing just over 2,700 people.

It was not until March 1945, that Allied forces at last crossed the Rhine. Meanwhile, the Red Army had nearly completed its sweep from the East. On 30 April 1945, with the fall of Berlin to Soviet forces imminent, Hitler committed suicide. VE – Victory in Europe – Day was declared as 8 May, the day after the German Supreme Command surrendered. On 15 August, after the atom bombs on Hiroshima and Nagasaki had broken stubborn Japanese resistance, VJ Day was celebrated. In between the victory days, the British had held a General Election. Civilians at home voted on 5 July, but announcement of results was delayed for three weeks while votes of service personnel overseas were collected. They came in a stupefying rush, revealing almost at once that Churchill and his Conservatives had lost in a landslide to Clement Attlee's Labour Party. Those who voted Labour believed that Churchill might be a great war leader but was not the man to give them what politicians told them was their just reward for their war effort – new houses, full employment, a National Health Service and improved Social Security. Attlee's triumph was taken to emphasise the fact that the British as a whole had won what had been called 'the People's War'.

OVERLEAF: **The Prime Minister visits the front at Caen, 22 July 1944.**

General Sir Bernard Montgomery, Commander of the 21st Army Group, is showing Churchill positions on a Map held by Lieutenant-General Sir Miles Dempsey, Commander of the British 2nd Army. Caen had been an immediate objective of British and Canadian troops on D-Day, 6 June, but deep into July the Germans held on to it, denying access to the plain stretching southward for 18 miles to Falaise. Montgomery turned to heavy bombers for help. On 7 July, bombers wreaked havoc in Caen and the Germans withdrew from the northern part of the city. Dempsey suggested a drive to Falaise, code-name GOODWOOD, which was launched on 18 July, but called off by Montgomery on the 20th after stubborn German resistance had been aided by a heavy thunderstorm. By then the British had lost more than a third of the tanks they had brought to Normandy. So the men in this photograph had reason to look worried.

FOLLOWING PAGE: **Heavy guns pound enemy positions, July 1944, Normandy, Caen front.**

German resistance in and beyond Caen after D-Day was particularly frustrating. Captain Malindine took this photo of a crew from 53 Heavy Regiment, loading a 55 mm gun under camouflage netting. This was an American weapon, commonly manned by British troops in France. It could fire a shell of 43.1 kg, 23,220 meters, at 853 m/sec. Over half of all battle casualties in World War II were caused by artillery fire rather than by tanks or aeroplanes, which we tend to imagine were by then dominant.

HOME FRONT

ONE OF THE criticisms aimed at Chamberlain's Government early in the war was that it was not mobilising the British people with sufficient fairness and thoroughness. The entry of the Labour Party into Churchill's Coalition Government eliminated the suspicions of many trade unionists. That summer the Government took comprehensive powers over all workers and all industries. Strikes were prohibited where the mechanisms of collective bargaining existed. The famous 'Dunkirk Spirit' exhibited itself, as people worked long hours of overtime to produce aircraft and other munitions. In the long run, this was counterproductive in two ways. Exhausted workers were less efficient and the habit of getting high overtime pay would widen the huge gap between men in the army who received very little and their contemporaries in 'reserved occupations'. Skilled men, including miners, were retained for the home front.

An engineer in the aircraft industry, would be earning very high wages while his former schoolfellow in the army would hear, that on the meagre government allowance, his wife was struggling even to feed and clothe their child.

That said the war reduced and up to a point eliminated social deprivation. High unemployment had been a nightmare in the Thirties. The drafting of so many men into the army quickly produced conditions of 'full employment'. By mid-1941 there was an acute manpower shortage. The Government accepted that everyone between 18 and 60 should now be obliged to undertake essential war work so that fit young men could be released from such tasks as Civil Defence. On 2 December 1941, the conscription of women between 20 and 30 was introduced. They were now driven into the women's services attached to the armed forces, or into work in 'war industry' or agriculture. Government propaganda continued to emphasise the 'volunteer' spirit which had prompted heroic dedication by many – though not all – civil defence workers during the Blitz. In practice compulsion was deemed essential, and war industry, by the middle of the war, was afflicted with an epidemic of unofficial strikes. But the good news was that everyone who wanted to earn money could do so, indeed *had to* do so.

Though the levels of provision offered under rationing now seem pitifully small – less than a pound of meat per person per week by August 1942, only two ounces of cheese in April 1944 – food control involved levelling up as well as levelling down. Free milk for all schoolchildren from the summer of 1940, was an innovation of stupendous consequence. By 1943, consumption of milk overall had risen by 30%, of potatoes by more than 40%, of other vegetables by 30%. Consumption of sugar and syrups was down by nearly a third. Meat-eating was down by 20%, that of poultry and fish by 40%. It was unfortunate that 40% less fruit was eaten – oranges were now rare, bananas wholly unobtainable. But the nation's diet, while stodgier, was sound and abundant. People were in that sense better fed, thanks to the exhaustive and exhausting efforts of British farmers. People might spend hours queuing for tinned salmon or tomatoes but this was less significant, in the long run, than the fact that superior nutrition was now available to the children of what had been the poorest families. Clothes rationing was an affliction only for those previously able to afford fancy dressing. Likewise, when a shortage of furniture, much needed by those bombed out of their homes, prompted the Government to sponsor new 'Utility' designs, the results were cheap, simple, aesthetically acceptable, and very durable.

At the peak of war effort, in 1944, UK population stood at 47,500,000. Of these, nearly five million were in the Armed Forces and the women's auxiliary services. In civil employment, the total of male workers was more than 2,000,000 down since 1940, to 10,347,000; that of women was up, from 5,306,000 to 6,620,000. Just as significant as the total figures was the shift of women workers from domestic service to industry. The era when even a young couple on a modest middle class income would automatically hire domestic help was over for ever. It is widely believed that the war furthered the emancipation of women, though this must be qualified by the fact that the birth-rate, declining before the war, rose sharply, and that it is clear that women in boring assembly line jobs commonly yearned for the moment when husbands in the army would return and they could settle in the role of housewives.

Employment in agriculture had increased though by nothing like the same ratio as that in metals, engineering, vehicles, shipbuilding, chemicals, explosives and paints – 'war industry' – where the rise since 1940 was from 3,500,000 to 5,000,000. The other great rise was in bureaucracy – employment in national and local government surging up to 1,809,000. Though the threat of invasion had long disappeared, the part-time Home Guard, now seen largely as a training facility for the army, had risen from 1,500,000 to 1,750,000. Industries serving consumers – textiles and clothing, boots and shoes, food, drink and tobacco, building and civil engineering – had lost huge proportions of their workforces. The big non-success story was mining. Numbers employed fell by less than ten percent, production of coal by much more.

As a result of all these shifts of effort, production of aircraft rose from 15,000 in 1940 to 26,500 in 1944, and the combined structure weight of the latter was three and a half times as great. Production of small arms ammunition had increased more than tenfold. More naval vessels of all sizes were being built and arable land in use had increased from 13,203,000 acres to 17,936,000. To the efforts of farmers aided by 'landgirls' were added those of people growing vegetables, and keeping pigs and poultry in gardens and allotments, 'digging for victory'.

In principle, people in wartime Britain had almost no spare time but they still flocked to cinemas, and listened avidly to radio. The BBC enjoyed its 'finest hour', providing, without competition, news, comedy, music and surreptitious education to the attentive nation.

OVERLEAF: **Women working in a Lancashire factory on 20mm cannon shells for the Ministry of Supply.**

The factory was located in underground tunnels at New Brighton pleasure beach, in suburban Liverpool. These tunnels had been discovered when foundations for a Fun Palace were being excavated. They were initially used as air shelters – Merseyside was bombed with special severity in the spring of 1941 – then converted to a space in which more than 100 people worked for the Government's Ministry of Supply which, as its name suggested, provided munitions for the armed forces. By the middle of the war, the best British fighter planes – the Spitfire, the Beaufighter, the Mosquito and the Hawker Typhoon which succeeded the Hurricane – were fitted with 20mm cannons which could pierce Luftwaffe armour as 0.303 machine gun fire could not.

FOLLOWING PAGE: **Submarine HMS Tribune, September 1942.**

British submarines, while not as fast as German US or Soviet counterparts were dependable and sufficiently armed. 'T' Class submarines, like this one, displaced 1571 tons and could proceed at over 15 mph on the surface, 8.7 mph under water. They had a range of 11,000 nautical miles. Commander

Edward Young, DSO, DSC, whose book *One of Our Submarines* (1952) was a post-war bestseller, was First Lieutenant in the lighter and slower 'S' Boat, *HMS Saracen*. He describes how, earlier in 1942, when on a training run out of Dunoon on the Clyde, the man at the periscope spotted a U-Boat surfacing less than a mile away. There was frantic action: – 'with the pumping and flooding order instrument under my hand, I had to cope with the change of trim caused by the men rushing aft the control room. Water must be put in for'ard and pumped out amidships'. The captain must not be unsighted by sinking below pericope depth, yet *Saracen* must not give its presence away by breaking surface. After two minutes, six torpedoes were released in quick succession. A tremendous explosion followed. In the midst of oil fuel spreading over the sea debris bobbing over the surface, just three Germans appeared. One was dead. Another deliberately sank under the water to evade capture. The third 'groaning dementedly and vomiting sea-water and oil' was pulled into the *Saracen*. 'Here he became conscious for a brief moment, long enough to open his eyes and look at me straight with an appaling expression of despair and hatred...' Set to work on cleaning duties, however, he eventually performed 'willingly and well...altogether a model prisoner'.

THE BATTLE OF THE ATLANTIC

I F T H E Battle of Britain in retrospect was decisive – as the first point at which the all-conquering Nazi war-thrust was halted – Britain could not have survived without winning the Battle of the Atlantic. This was conducted not only by the Royal Navy but by legions of merchant seamen and the unsung Coastal Command of the RAF. Over 30,000 merchant seamen died.

Even after the conquest of France and Scandinavia had given Germany advanced bases, German naval power on the surface of the sea was incapable of inflicting serious damage on the traffic between Britain and the New World which provided essential food and munitions, and later conveyed huge numbers of GIs. But U-Boat submarines, in their 'wolfpacks', posed a very serious challenge, from the first day of war, when one sank the liner *Athenia* off the Hebrides under the misapprehension that it was a Royal Navy vessel. In the crucial winter of 1940-1, the Germans had too few U-Boats – only 21 in February – to exploit Britain's crisis fully. By the early summer of 1941, the

British had cracked the U-Boats' cypher system, and even before Pearl harbour, the USA was actively engaged in protecting shipping. After the US entered the war, U-Boats briefly enjoyed spectacular success along the eastern seaboard of North America, and Allied merchant shipping losses peaked in 1942. In the winter of 1942-3, the UK faced its most serious import crisis of the war as the Battle of the Atlantic reached a climax, with over 400 U-boats operational, and over 100 at sea at any given time, mostly in the Atlantic. In early March, all North Atlantic convoys were located by the Germans, half were attacked, and over one-fifth of vessels in these convoys were sunk. But the Allies responded with more aircraft, escort carriers and more destroyers. 47 U-Boats went to the bottom in May, and at the end of that month the decimated 'wolfpacks' were withdrawn. Allied losses from January through May 1943 had averaged 450,000 tons a month, mostly due to U-Boats. Over the last seven months of the year, only about 50,000 tons a month were lost through submarine action. The Battle of the Atlantic had been won.

LEFT: **A woman of the Auxiliary Territorial Service at an anti-aircraft gunsite, December 1942.**

A 3.7 AA gun is in the background. The women's section of the Army had been formed in 1939, initially from volunteers. Numbers rose from 24,000 to a peak of 212,500 in September 1943, when the Women's Royal Naval Service had 60,000 'Wrens' – still rising – and there were 180,000 'Waffs' in the Auxiliary Air Force. The role of 'Ats' was especially significant in anti-aircraft duties, where they did everything except actually fire the guns. Large numbers of women fought with the Red Army, often with conspicuous ferocity, but the Western Allies recoiled from the idea of women in combat. If this photograph was taken in Britain, its 'At' was sharing an exceptionally tedious war – there were few serious German raids on the island between the early summer of 1941 and the brief 'Little Blitz' of London in February 1944 which was followed later that year by VI flying bombs. The poet Gavin Ewart went on record saying that: 'My spell as an officer in a Light Anti-Aircraft Regiment, engaged on the air defence of factories and airfields in the UK, was one of the dullest and most boring periods of my whole life.'

OVERLEAF: **Naval gunners, November 1943.**

A 'pom pom' gun with its crew, posed with exceptional skill and care.

BURMA CAMPAIGN

In WHAT WAS nicknamed 'the forgotten war', the British Imperial army fought its longest single campaign against the Japanese in Burma from December 1941 to August 1945. Most of the troops in General Slim's ultimately victorious Fourteenth Army were Indians or other Asians, and black troops from Africa played a notable part. Participants from the UK believed rightly that the public at home had its eyes trained on the Middle East, and later Europe, and paid scant attention to their sufferings and exploits.

In February 1942, the rapid Japanese advance through southeast Asia culminated in the capture, by 35,000 soldiers confronted with a much larger Imperial force, of the key British Imperial fortress of Singapore. 14,000 Australians, 16,000 Britons and 32,000 Indians passed into Japanese captivity. Many of the Indian troops joined the Indian National Army created by the Japanese and ostensibly dedicated to achieving independence for the Sub-Continent. Burma was now the stepping stone to India for the Japanese, who granted the country nominal independence in 1943, after they had successfully blocked the only remaining supply route to China, where they waged brutal war against Chiang Kai Shek's Nationalists and Mao Tse Tung's Communist guerrillas. By May 1942. British forces had retreated to India and the Japanese controlled the whole of Burma.

The turning point came in March 1944. General Mutaguchi, leading the Fifteen Japanese Army and the new INA, struck into Assam in north-east India and suffered, at Imphal, the worst defeat in Japanese military history. Nevertheless, the Japanese were stubborn. It was not until May 1945 that Slim's forces recaptured the Burmese capital, Rangoon. Fought in mountains, through thick jungles and over wide rivers, this campaign gave Britons engaged in it experiences utterly unlike those found elsewhere. Some of the Africans fighting alongside them went back to their villages with the message that their British masters were men, like others, who could be opposed and shot up by people of other races.

LEFT: **Assam, India, January 1942. A convoy of trucks carrying men of the Royal Engineers to Imphal wait at the traffic gates at Mao on the Dimapur-Kohima road.** Imphal, south of Kohima, was a key base for the British, close to the frontier of Burma which the Japanese were at this time overrunning. British Imperial troops would fare badly against them. In March, General William Slim would take over as commander, and lead what was left of them back to India, in the longest fighting retreat in British military history. Colour photographs from the Burmese front are rare, and it is not clear why this one would have been taken.

DAYS IN UNIFORM –
LIFE AND DEATH IN THE FORCES

B EFORE THE 'Industrial Revolution' of the 18th and 19th centuries, and the coincidental rise of State bureaucracies, most people knew and could explain what most other people did. New technologies, 'division of labour', urbanisation and sheer increase in population conspired to reverse this. The general process affected the armed forces, as conscription in the 20th century created vast forces with many specialist arms. Victory still depended, as in most ancient times, on occupying with foot-soldiers, territory taken from the enemy. But behind the 'PBI' – the 'Poor Bloody Infantry' – an ever-increasing tail of support personnel stretched back to the offices where desk-soldiers attempted to control events with the help now of radio and of information derived from cracked codes. Meanwhile friendly aircraft roared overhead, above marching men, supplementing or replacing ground-based artillery or attacking enemy aircraft sent in with similar aims and prone to bomb or strafe the PBI. Granted the size and complexity of the armed forces and the geographical spread of the war, experiences of men and women in uniform differed enormously. Between the end of the Dunkirk evacuation in June 1940 and D-Day four years later, a very high proportion at any one time were languishing in Britain, subject, from an officer class still drawn from the social elite, to orders which were often of the kind which the PBI characterised as 'bullshit'. They got little pay and were envious of more glamourous characters in RAF and RN uniforms, not to speak of sleek GIs. At an extreme, small groups of men tended isolated Anti-Aircraft gunposts in the English countryside. Those sent abroad might have interesting experiences without running the slightest risk of death except by accident — training native troops in Nigeria for instance, or mending army vehicles in the Sudan.

At another extreme was life in Bomber Command. Of 125,000 men flying in bombers, 55,000 died, and when prisoners of war and men wounded were added, the total casualty rate was 60%. Flying night after night over Germany, young men would gradually lose most of their comrades. Risks on the Arctic Convoy were not quite so extreme, but the men who escorted merchant ships to the Soviet ports of Murmansk, Archangel and Molotovsk through the Norwegian and Barents seas from 21 August 1941, to 16 April 1945, were in severe jeopardy in an extreme climate, supplying Britain's Red allies with nearly a quarter of all their Lend-Lease supplies from the US.

One terrain in particular belonged to the Empire's soldiers. It stretched from Syria and Palestine through Libya and eventually included Tunisia, where American troops briefly got in on the act. It embraced the ancient, cosmopolitan and corrupt cities of Egypt, nominally an independent country, in fact under Imperial control. The apparatus of the Eighth Army had ample room for men in safe desk jobs as well as tank men and infantry fighting across the almost unpeopled desert. This was the antithesis of the First World War's attrition in the trenches, as tanks swept victoriously across acre after arid acre, only to be chased back again. Australians, then British, Polish and South African troops were besieged in the Libyan port of Tobruk by Rommel, and withstood German attacks from early 1941 until 20 June 1942, when the town's capture seemed almost as sore a blow to the Empire as the fall of Singapore – nearly all the 35,000 Imperial troops in Tobruk became prisoners of war.

Though Canadians did not feature here, except as airmen, the Empire as a collective entity was engaged as nowhere else. Three Indian Divisions fought in North Africa. So did the sole New Zealand Division, the 'Div', whom Rommel thought the best soldiers of the lot, though this would have been hotly contested by the 51st Highland Division from Scotland. It was out of North African experience that two Scots, Hamish Henderson and Sorley Maclean, wrote poetry of a quality unmatched in other theatres, though rivalled by an Englishman, Keith Douglas, whose 'Cairo Jag' contrasts the city to the territory a day's travel to the west;

...a new world

the vegetation is of iron

dead tanks, gun barrels split like celery

the metal brambles have no flowers or berries

and there are all sorts of manure, you can imagine

the dead themselves, their boots, clothes and possessions

clinging to the ground, a man with no head

has a packet of chocolate and a souvenir of Tripoli.

LEFT: **After the inauguration of new Regents in San Marino, 1 October, 1944.**

San Marino, a territory of 24 square miles, has its own national football team, Formula One Grand Prix, and postage stamps — a valuable export. It is allegedly the oldest republic in the world, founded, according to legend, by Marinus in the middle of the fourth century BC. In 1862, it came under the 'protection' of the new Kingdom of Italy. It claimed neutrality in World War II, but was severely bombed just the same. The arrival of the Allies got rid of the regime imposed by Mussolini, and San Marino reverted to its free tradition, whereby a general council of 60 elected by proportional representation with universal male suffrage — women got the vote only in 1958 — passed laws, and an executive of twelve implemented them. Two *capitani reggenti* or regents were elected as heads of state every six months, on 1 April and 1 October. This photograph shows civilians and members of the British Army Film and Photographic Corps in the main square after such an election. The Corps consisted of men who had received special training. Most had been press photographers before joining the army. Captain Tanner took this particular shot, and others towards the end of this book. Supplies of American Kodak colour film had come in with the GIs after the US entered the war in December 1941.

PHOTOGRAPHY AT WAR

T HE POTENCY OF celluloid in propaganda was well understood in 1939. Just as the British film industry willingly worked with the Ministry of Information to produce features with wholesome propaganda aims, and fine documentaries, so the leading illustrated magazine, *Picture Post*, offered wholehearted cooperation from the outset. Its ace photographer Bert Hardie produced some of the most memorable images of the Blitz. So did the less warm-hearted but technically awesome Bill Brandt, working directly for the Government. It was an inevitable condition of total war that no image could be published which might generate despondency, so that pictures of civilians being rescued from the ruins of their houses, if they were not in some way cheerful, would have a quality akin to famous paintings of the sufferings of Christ.

A well-to-do woman called Rosie Newman happened to have some colour film in 1940. As a rank amateur, she filmed Blitz scenes in colour. Her footage surprises us because her images are neither posed nor composed. Civil Defence workers at a scene where a bomb has fallen look, in the middle distance, much like men in peacetime demolishing a house or mending a road. Colour film was in short supply in Britain, more so than in Germany or in the USA, where the colour movie *Gone With The Wind* was the great hit as war broke out in Europe. Colour pictures were not printed by the British press. Britain's war has come down to us in black and white.

Most of the pictures in this book are the work of official 'war photographers' in the years 1942-1945. It followed from wartime conditions that colour photographs, special not normal items, would usually be taken to give a positive, noble glow to the war effort. We will not see civilians 'trekking' forlornly out of bombed towns, exhausted bomber crews getting savagely drunk, good-time girls jiving with GIs or the burnt-out tanks and corpses of the North African desert as evoked by Douglas and other poets. We will see impressive hardware and calm service personnel. That said, to perceive such things in colour is to cut through black and white nostalgia to the actual sunshine in which our fathers and grandfathers fought and their wives struggled.

OVERLEAF: **April 1941, Supermarine Spitfire Mark II, P7895 'PN-N' of 72 Squadron based at Acklington in flight over the coast.**

Acklington is in Northumberland. The pilot here is Flight Lieutenant R.Deacon Elliott. The Spitfire was Britain's most glamorous warplane. The slower but sturdy Hawker Hurricane shot down plenty of Germans in the Battle of Britain and experts will argue forever about whether the Spitfire was superior to its Luftwaffe rival, the Messerschmitt Bf 109E-3. Flown to its maximum, arguably it was. Designed by Reginald Mitchell, who died before he could see it in action, the Spitfire in 1940 was the plane that all the ambitious young pilots yearned to fly. But Hurricanes outnumbered Spitfires in Fighter Command during the Battle of Britain. During the Battle an improved Mark II Spitfire, as shown here, began to arrive, incorporating lessons learned in combat. It was faster and had better armour, 29ft 9in in length, with a wing span of 36ft 10in. Its Rolls Royce Merlin XII engine generated 1236hp. It was armed with eight Browning machine guns. Its maximum speed, possible at 17,550 feet was 354 mph. (The Messerschmitt Bf 109E-3 achieved exactly the same maximum at 12,300 feet. The Hurricane Mk I couldn't get above 316 mph.)

FOLLOWING PAGE: **1942. A machine gunner on an escort vessel keeps watch as the Royal Navy guards a British convoy across the Atlantic.**

1942 was a crucial year in the Battle of the Atlantic (See Introduction). The offensive pose of this keen gunner is reassuring. The fact was that battleships, once kings of the sea, were in this war now doubly vulnerable, to submarines lurking below the surface, and aircraft, which could be launched from carriers, attacking from the sky.

FOLLOWING PAGE: **Groundcrew refuelling a Short Stirling Mark 1, N 1601, of No 1651 Heavy Conversion Unit from an AEC 6x6 petrol tanker at Waterbeach, 29 April 1942.**

The Stirling was not a very good plane. The RAF ordered it as a heavy bomber in 1939. The prototype crashed on its maiden flight in 1939. So no Stirlings were delivered till August 1940, and the plane did not feature in operations till February 1941. It was a disappointment. It couldn't fly as high as was desirable for offensive flying and its bombload over long distances was smallish. Lots of Stirlings flew sorties over Germany, but they could not match the performance of the Halifax and the Lancaster. Their range — under 600 miles — was less than half that of either. This specimen was photographed in Cambridgeshire.

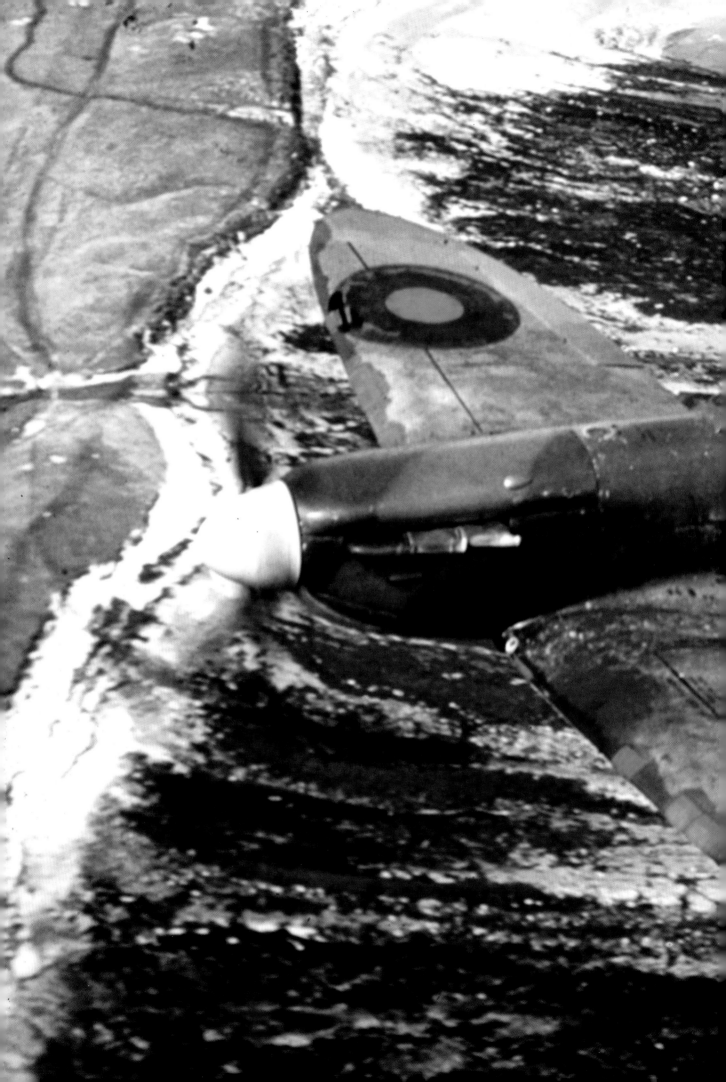

OVERLEAF: **On the bridge of the aircraft carrier HMS Formidable off the North African coast, 1942 – officers and men observing landing beaches.**

Formidable looked as if she would live up to her name. She was nearly 750 feet long and over 30 yards across. She carried a crew of 1,500 and thirty-odd planes. But that was not enough planes to defend her adequately under attack from land-based German planes in the Mediterranean, where she participated in the struggle to get supplies to the besieged i sland of Malta, and was badly mauled in May 1941. Here, however, two crewman are watching a successful operation – the Allied landings in Algeria of November 1942 which swiftly brought surrender from the Vichy French.

FOLLOWING PAGE: **An RAF Lockheed Hudson of the Middle East Communications Flight above the Pyramids in Egypt, Summer 1942.**

Hudsons served in almost every theatre of the maritime war. These Hudsons however, are not on offensive operations.

FOLLOWING PAGE: **1942. An RAF aircrew holds a carrier pigeon beside a Lockheed Hudson of Coastal Command.**

The Hudson, an American import, was never quite a household name, yet it was a most successful and highly versatile plane. It was converted from a civil airliner, the Electra. In one of these the sinister tycoon, Howard Hughes, flew round the world in four days. Another conveyed Neville Chamberlain to meet Hitler in Munich in September 1938. Meanwhile, the British had ordered 250 Hudson bombers for the RAF. These were promptly delivered at the relatively modest cost of $100,000 each. Coastal Command had its first Hudson squadron by the summer of 1939. Four more soon followed. After war broke out, nearly 3,000 Hudsons were built for Imperial and Allied air forces. Following various design improvements, the Mark IV was capable of 284 mph and had a range of 2,160 miles at a cruising speed of 220 mph. The RAF ultimately had 17 Hudson squadrons. While Hudsons performed many tasks, including sorties against Germany, reconnaissance and transport, they won special glory as anti-submarine specialists in the Battle of the Atlantic. They disposed of 25 U-boats.

LEFT: **On a British warship, 1942.**

The sailor on watch wears a duffel coat and steel helmet. A Pom Pom gun is in the foreground.

OVERLEAF: **On board submarine HMS Tribune, September 1942.**

Leading Seaman Walker on the bridge, is keeping a look out with a torpedo night sight.

FOLLOWING PAGE: **Forward view from the conning tower of submarine HMS Tribune, 1942.**

The submarine is running along the surface in Scottish waters. Submarines dived only when necessary – though by this stage of the war German U-boats had been driven almost permanently undersea in areas covered by centimetric Allied airborne radar.

OVERLEAF: **September 1942, three Avro Lancaster B Mark I's of No.44 Squadron RAF, flying above the clouds.**

The Avro Lancaster, operational from March 1942, was Bomber Command's prime aircraft, with a top speed approaching 300 mph, a range of 1,660 miles and a bombload of up to 22,000 lb. 7,377 were built. This squadron was based at Waddington in Lincolnshire. Left to right, we see W4125 flown by Sergeant Colin Watt, W4162 flown by Pilot Officer T.G.Hackney and W187 flown by Pilot Officer J.D.V.S. Stephens DFM. Watt was part of the Australian contingent in Bomber Command. The fates of the other two exemplify the Command's horrific casualty rate. Hackney was later killed while serving with No.83 squadron. Stephens and his crew died just two days after this photograph was taken during a raid on Wismar in Germany. On the night of 1 October, Bomber Command initiated three small raids, to Flensburg, Lubeck and Wismar. Weather conditions were difficult and the Pathfinder planes which normally now flew ahead to mark targets with incendiaries were not employed. 78 Lancasters from 5 Group scattered bombs around

Wismar. Two failed to return. At this time casualty rates in Bomber Command were causing great concern. Aircrew were expected to complete a first tour of 30 operations, then, after a rest, come back for another 20. With casualty rates in the autumn of 1942 at 4.6 percent, the chances of a man surviving fifty operations were one in ten, or lower. Morale, not surprisingly, was falling...

FOLLOWING PAGE: **Paratroop training, Netheravon, Wiltshire, October 2 1942.**

A Whitley of 295 squadron, is the plane involved. One of the massive ironies of the great British war effort was that men and women often worked overtime to produce poor, or even useless models. The Whitleys were not very good bombing planes, manufactured in huge numbers, but withdrawn from operations over Germany in 1942. The plane shown here is one of those converted to drop parachutists from a hole in the floor.

OVERLEAF: **Paratrooper training in Britain, October 2 1942.**

Early in the war, following their use by the Germans in front of drives into Scandinavia and the Low Countries, paratroopers were expected to play a major role (there were delirious rumours in Britain of Germans dropping disguised as nuns). Paras did count – for instance on D Day, June 6 1944, descending in Normandy to secure tank positions ahead of the men landing on the beaches. They were not going to be successful without infantry coming up swiftly in support. The Royal Navy prevented reinforcement by sea of the Germans dropped on Crete in May,1942. In the absence of RAF defences, the Germans had total control of the air. Though a tactical blunder by one New Zealand commander enabled them to capture one of the island's three airbases, and swiftly after that to chase the British Empire troops in retreat, German losses were so severe – about a quarter of their parachutists – that no similar operation was sanctioned thereafter. The British had not learnt the lesson of Crete. On September 17, 1944, General Montgomery dropped 16,500 paratroopers and 3,500 troops in gliders on

Arnhem in the Netherlands, with the aim of seizing eight key bridges and speeding up allied advance towards Germany. They ran into two SS Panzer Divisions, refitting in the area, who had just completed an exercise on how to deal with airborne landings. Advancing allied land forces were held up. By 25 September, the operation was abandoned, after heavy casualties, with 6,000 prisoners of war left in German hands.

FOLLOWING PAGE: **Paratrooper on manoeuvres in Britain.**

In the face of resistance from army commanders who resented losing able soldiers eager to volunteer for airborne warfare, Churchill ensured the creation of a parachute brigade of three battalions. British paratroops carried, beside light equipment, Sten machine carbines weighing 6.4 lb and capable of firing 550 rounds per minute. With these, they could go into action at once.

LEFT: **Paratroop jump from a static balloon.**

The practice of dropping paratroop trainees from balloons continued till the 1960s. The first taste of jumping was remarkable for trainees. Some found taking the plunge unendurably scary, but in his great novel *Sword of Honour* (1965), based mostly on his own war memories, Evelyn Waugh describes the feelings of his protagonist, Guy Crouchback, on his first jump: 'He experienced rapture, something as near as his earthbound soul could reach to as a foretaste of paradise... As though he had cast the constraining bounds of flesh and muscle and nerve, he found himself floating free; the harness that had so irked him in the narrow, dusky, resounding carriage now almost imperceptibly supported him. He was a free spirit in an element as fresh as on the day of its creation.' It is not clear when and where this 'blimp' – barrage balloon – is being used for training. The basic function of such balloons, tethered to the ground with wire cables, was to make things difficult for low-flying enemy aircraft. Thousands were used in Britain, often handled by women under RAF Balloon Command. They had successes during the Blitz of 1940-1, and in 1944-5 they destroyed 231 V1 flying bombs. By day, their portly presence over British cities was almost comic. At night, lit up by searchlights and the flames of huge fires, they achieved an eerie kind of beauty.

OVERLEAF: **Prime Minister Churchill, with the Lord Privy Seal, Sir Stafford Cripps, and the Commander-in-Chief, Home Fleet, Sir John Tovey, on the quarterdeck of HMS King George V, at Scapa Flow, 11 October 1942.**

Scapa Flow, in the Orkney island of Hoy, was a remote but very important base for the Royal Navy, whose personnel might find it nightmarish to be isolated in a place with lots of seals, skuas and puffins but very few people. No doubt the visit represented here was designed to boost morale. Tovey (1885-1971) was a distinguished sailor, knighted in 1941, the year in which his Home Fleet warships sank the German battleship *Bismarck*. Cripps (1889-1962) was a lawyer of aristocratic background who had converted to Socialism between the wars and had been expelled from the Labour Party for advocating a popular front with Communists against Nazism. He had served as Ambassador to Moscow from 1940 to 1942, and came home with all the prestige of the valiant Soviet ally as his aura. He was seen by many as a possible rival to Churchill, who disliked him, not just for that reason, but because Cripps's pious Christian austerity jarred against his own uninhibited enjoyment of brandy and cigars. However, he was given a place in the War Cabinet as Lord Privy Seal. Churchill, who had begun the war as First Lord of the Admiralty, greatly enjoyed posing, as here, in his sailor's hat. Cripps' unassuming scarf and nervous grin – or grimace – express a very different personality.

OVERLEAF: **The crew of a Churchill tank, from A Squadron 43rd Battalion Royal Tank Regiment, 33rd Brigade, discuss operations around a map while on manoeuvres in Britain, October 1942.**

The Germans named their best 'tanks' – Tracked Armoured Fighting Vehicles – after animals: the panther and tiger; the Americans, after heroes of former wars – Grant, Sherman, Pershing. The British recklessly gave the name of their great war leader to their latest model. This might have seemed especially appropriate since, as First Lord of the Admiralty, Churchill – a devotee of the futuristic writings of HG Wells – had given decisive encouragement to the development of the tank in Britain during the First World War. Trundling at walking pace over the devastated Western Front, tanks had then made an extraordinary visual impression but no epochal military impact. In the second, when the fastest models could go at well over

30 mph, tanks were deployed outflanking static defences or fighting huge pitched battles in Germany's invasion of France, in the North African desert, and on the vast plains of the Soviet Union. Unfortunately, Britain had lost its early lead in tank design.

This is a Mark 11 Churchill. Mark I had arrived in service in 1941. 24 feet, 5 inches long, heavily armoured, with a crew of five, the Churchill could reach 17 mph. Its inadequacy was exposed by Rommel. It was inferior to German tanks, though these in turn were bested by the finest Soviet products. The Mark VII Churchill (1944) was heavier and slower than its predecessors.

OVERLEAF: **A crashed German Junkers Ju 52 Troop Carrier on Gabes airfield in North Africa on the day of its occupation by the Allies, May 1943.**

Gabes, in the south of Tunisia, fell while Montgomery's Eighth Army was advancing to join Americans engaged against Germans in that country since the previous November. After very fierce resistance, Rommel's men succumbed in mid-May.

FOLLOWING PAGE: **Goubine, Tunisia, May 1943. Flight Lieutenant W.T.I. Pentland of no 417 Squadron Royal Canadian Air Force, waits to start up his Spitfire Mark V (BR 195/AR-T).**

The RCAF contributed 48 squadrons and 94,000 officers and men to the Imperial war effort. Over 17,000 of these were killed. The bombing offensive in Europe was the chief focus of RCAF activity, but as this photograph shows, its pilots also flew in the Mediterranean and North Africa. The Spitfire Mark V was already being superseded by Marks 9 (from 1942) and 12 (1943). Its top speed (374mph) was marginally faster than the model which flew in the Battle of Britain, but it was achieved at a lower altitude. It carried cannon as well as machine guns. Its successors touched 400 mph and finally (Mark 14, 1944) 450 mph, after the Merlin engine had been replaced by the Griffon.

OVERLEAF: **The Viceroy of India, Field Marshal Sir Archibald Wavell, GCB, CMG, MC, at his desk in 1943.**

Wavell (1883-1950) was a tough soldier and also a highly intelligent, sensitive man. He found it hard to hide his boredom on routine social occasions, but seized any chance to recite poetry from memory – he had an enormous stock of poems in his head, and his personal anthology *Other Men's Flowers* was a bestseller. He fought in the Boer War and lost an eye in the First World War. In July 1939 he became C-in-C of Middle East Command. This gave him the privilege of driving the Italians out of their North African colony, Cyrenaica, in 1940-1. But Churchill was furious when Wavell authorised troops defending British Somaliland against the Italians to evacuate in August 1940. He said the general involved should be sacked. Wavell cabled the Prime Minister that a big butcher's bill was not necessarily evidence of sound tactics. The two men never got on thereafter. In the new year, British attacks from the Sudan, Kenya and Aden crushed the Italians in East Africa and conquered their possessions there – Ethiopia, Eritrea, and Somaliland. Their commander surrendered on 16 May 1941 but that was Wavell's last good fortune. Choice troops sent to the Balkans were forced into retreat. British Imperial forces, beaten through Greece across to Crete, were expelled or captured by June. The arrival of Rommel to command his Afrika Korps in the desert was a prelude to British retreat, and there was trouble in Iraq and Syria. In July 1941, Churchill replaced Wavell with General Auchinleck, and sent him to India as C-in-C. Posted to Java in the Netherlands East Indies in January 1942, he promptly had to pull out in face of the unstoppable Japanese. Nor, back in India, could he halt the Japanese conquest of Burma. In October 1943, he was made Viceroy of India as a stopgap till the end of the war. His admiration of the great Nationalist leader Gandhi was useful, though distasteful to Churchill – in 1944, Wavell released the Mahatma from prison on grounds of ill health – but he presided over the disastrous, man-made Bengal famine of 1943, in which more than 3,000,000 people died. He came near to resolving the conflict between Hindu and Muslim nationalists which, through partition, produced Pakistan at the moment in 1947, after Wavell had handed over his post to Mountbatten, when the sub-continent was finally freed from British rule.

LEFT: **Admiral Lord Louis Mountbatten, 1943.**

Born Prince Louis of Battenberg, a grandson of Queen Victoria, Mountbatten (1900-1979) was known as 'Dickie' to his many friends. His father, First Sea Lord in 1914, was hounded out of office because of his German name, hence anglicisation to 'Mountbatten' in 1917. 'Dickie' saw action with the Navy in the First World War, and began the Second as a destroyer captain. His dashing but erratic career in this capacity ended in 1941 when his ship was sunk by German aircraft off Crete. But the Americans liked this handsome, high profile chap, and Churchill made him chief of Combined Operations in October 1941. His biggest operation, the cross-Channel raid on Dieppe in August 1942, was an unmitigated disaster, but his career was unaffected, and in August 1943, having just been promoted, the youngest Admiral in RN history, he was made Supreme Commander of the newly created South East Asia Command. As such, he took the final Japanese surrender at Singapore on 12 September 1945, going on to become the last British Viceroy of India. Hardly a great fighting officer or strategist, he was a charmer, a diplomat, and a good organiser.

RIGHT: **General Sir Bernard Montgomery, 29 May 1943.**

Taken during a trip back to Britain from the Mediterranean theatre where his Eighth Army had just chased Rommel out of Africa, this shows 'Monty' (1887-1976) wearing the 'battle sweater' and tank officer's beret which were part of his image. This man of Scots-Irish stock was privately – at times publicly – the most egotistical of commanders, yet he cultivated the common touch and won the affectionate loyalty of ordinary soldiers. Badly wounded in 1914, so that he served thereafter as a staff officer, he soldiered in India and the Middle East between the wars, then created an impression as commander of the 3rd Division of the British Expeditionary Force which retreated through France to Dunkirk in 1940. After a series of important appointments in Britain, he got the chance to command in Egypt after a succession of British generals had failed against Rommel. He rallied the Eighth Army and his gift for meticulous advance planning (some saw this as excessive caution) ensured the defeat of Rommel at El Alamein in October 1942. Promoted to General and knighted, he went on to command allied land operations in France after D-Day, infuriating his overall commander, Eisenhower, and other US generals by his cocksure conceit. Rather seriously racist, he was not a very pleasant man, and knowledge of his human flaws has undermined what, in 1942-1945, was a great military reputation and a very positive image with the British public.

OVERLEAF: **Sir Arthur Harris at his desk, June 29, 1943.**

Harris (1892-1984), Commander in Chief of RAF Bomber Command from 1942 to 1945, was the only officer of such seniority not to receive a peerage after the war in the victory honours list. His request for a special campaign medal for Bomber Command was also refused. This reflected revulsion amongst humane British leaders over the job which his men had done. He had fallen in with the policy, not originally his own, of 'area bombing'. The idea was that if you forgot about concentrating only on targets of military significance and flattened German cities and the homes in which workers lived, this would bring the Third Reich to its knees. After he became C-in-C in February 1942, he tested on the ancient Hanseatic ports of Lubeck and Rostock, his notion that incendiaries would destroy cities more effectively than high explosive bombs. He was gratified to notice how well medieval houses burnt. These operations provoked German retaliation in a series of 'Baedaker raids' against British cathedral cities. In May 1942, Harris took a huge risk when he called up every available plane in his command, including some from training units, to mount a 'thousand-bomber' raid on Cologne. This duly caused devastation, and prefigured later massive attacks on Berlin and Hamburg in particular. But Germany fought on, and actually increased war production steeply. Like the 'Blitz' of Britain, RAF raids if anything stiffened morale. Meanwhile, Bomber Command casualties were horrific. Harris went ahead regardless, till by the time of the notorious raid on Dresden in February 1945, even Churchill, formerly a strong supporter, recoiled from Harris's procedures. Yet this stubborn South African retained the loyalty of the men he led who, like him, after the war, became virtual pariahs.

OVERLEAF: **Churchill tank in Italy, 20 July 1944.**

For the Churchill, see page 100. This one is from B squadron of the 51st

Royal Tank Regiment. It is crawling through undergrowth somewhere

between Pescara and Rimini as the Eighth Army under General Alexander

drives hesitantly northwards along the Adriatic coast towards the Po river.

This photograph is not intended to symbolise the slowness of Allied

progress in Italy, but unintentionally does so very well. Fighting in Italy

continued right down to 2 May 1945.

FOLLOWING PAGE: **Liberation of Eindhoven, Netherlands, 20
September 1944.**

This was the first major Dutch town to be liberated by the Allies. The

people dancing in the streets here are probably singing some noble or

traditional song, but the far from jubilant look on their faces was prophetic.

As Montgomery's men pushed towards Germany, most of the Netherlands

remained in Nazi hands. On the last day of the war the Germans still held

the provinces of North and South Holland, including Rotterdam, the Hague

and Amsterdam. Civilians endured not only the ministrations of the

Gestapo, but acute food shortages over a terrible winter when many starved to death. Meanwhile, Eindhoven itself would be bombed by the Luftwaffe. The prominence of the colour orange in this picture will not surprise followers of international football. Orange is the colour of Netherlands fans in tribute to the royal house of Orange which has supplied monarchs since the 16th century. Chastened by news of the sufferings of her people, once-proud Queen Wilhelmina returned after five years in exile in London on 2 May 1945, with a 'court' consisting of her daughter and three aides. Her people flocked to pay tribute in person. Hoping for a renewal of Dutch national spirit, she told one aide: 'Best of all I would have liked to come back to Holland in the evening and then just ring a doorbell somewhere, at an ordinary house, or a farm perhaps, and then have asked the woman who opened the door, "May I spend the night here with you?" But in an exhausted and disillusioned country where over 90,000 people were at one point imprisoned for collaboration with the Nazis and many parties strove rancorously for political power, her dream faded, and she abdicated in 1948 in favour of her daughter, Juliana.

OVERLEAF: **Allied War Leaders meet at Yalta in the Crimea, February 1945.**

It is not clear from this photograph that both Churchill (seated left) and Stalin (right) were well below average height. That Roosevelt, seated between them, was mortally ill, is retrospectively visible. He died on 12 April, believing that agreements with the Soviet Union reached at Yalta would moderate that country's policy in the Eastern European lands it would dominate. The previous September he had made a secret deal with Churchill whereby knowledge of the new atomic bomb which was being developed would be restricted to their two nations. The Cold War would soon begin.

Behind the leaders stand the foreign ministers – left to right, Anthony Eden, British Foreign Secretary, Edward Stettinius, US Secretary of State, and Vlacheslav Molotov, Soviet Commissar for Foreign Affairs: diplomacy proposed and disposed. In return for entering, at last, the war against Japan, the Soviet Union would recover the southern part of Sakhalin Island, once part of the Tsarist Empire, and Mongolia would remain a Soviet satellite. It was agreed that all nationals accused of being deserters or traitors should be returned to their countries of origin. Over 4,000,000 opponents of Stalin's regime who had fought alongside the Germans would be repatriated. Officers would be shot; other ranks sent to the Gulag labour camps. Stalin, meanwhile, was letting Britain do what it liked to suppress Communist-led insurgency in Greece, where liberation proved to be the prelude to a savage civil war (1946-1949). 'Yalta' has become synonymous with 'betrayal'.

LEFT: **Corporal M. Smith of the Duke of Cornwall's Light infantry, posing with a 'Tommy gun' on the wall at the main headquarters of the 8th Army in the San Angelo area.**

Smith, a former metal polisher from Birmingham had served in North Africa before crossing into Italy in early 1944. He was no doubt relieved to have gone forward alive from the horrific fighting at Cassino. This photograph and the next one were taken by Captain Tanner. The Army Film and Photographic Unit consisted of men, given some training, who were often pre-war press photographers. Tanner certainly composes a very pretty shot here.

OVERLEAF: **British 8th Army troops cross the River Po, beyond Ferrara 28 April 1945.**

Tanner took this one to test the colour and definition of an uncommonly large lens with a focal length of 17 inches. German resistance in Italy is very nearly over. Two days from now Hitler will commit suicide in his bunker as Soviet troops overrun Berlin.

OVERLEAF: **VE Day in Whitehall, 8 May 1945**

In the historic centre of British Imperial administration, crowds gather in front of the Ministry of Health. Churchill addressed his victorious people from a balcony garnished with Allied flags, like the roof above. In the right foreground is the simple noble Cenotaph designed by Sir Edwin Lutyens as a monument to the dead of the First World War, 'Lest We Forget'. This photograph must have been taken while the vast throng was still building up as word went round that Churchill would speak at six pm. People shinned up lamposts and bus-stop signs to get a better view. Chants of 'We want Winnie!' were raised. When someone yelled 'Why don't 'e come out?', a wit shouted: "E's 'aving a drink dear!' When at last he emerged, puffing a cigar, he gave his trademark V sign and the cheering redoubled. 'This is your victory', he told them...'In all our long history we have never seen a greater day than this. Everyone, man or woman, has done their best. Everyone

has tried.' After he disappeared back into the Ministry, the crowd,

disciplined by years of queuing, dispersed in an orderly way. But when

Churchill returned for more speeches four hours later, the

atmosphere was uninhibited and Churchill enjoyed himself, as his

private secretary put it, 'like a schoolboy on an outing', eventually

leading about 30,000 people in the song 'Land of Hope and Glory'.

RIGHT: **VE Day.**

This picture may seem to speak for itself, but does not tell you that the photographer who took it, Graham Ray, was himself still in short trousers. The Lyons food firm was something of a national institution. Apart from manufacturing cakes and pies and purveying tea, coffee and cocoa sold by grocers, the company ran the famous Lyons Corner Houses in London, inexpensive places to sit with a bite and a cuppa, served by uniformed waitresses.

LEFT: **Klagenfurt area, occupied Austria, 17 May 1945**

The British Eighth Army, once heroes of desert war, now find life less hectic in the mountains of central Europe. The little girl, Anna, is four years old. These two soldiers of the Royal Military Police are billetted with her family. The one who's standing holds a Tyrolean pipe and beer in a typically Austrian mug. The photograph's message of reconciliation is clear. Austria, a German-speaking country, was not going to cleanse German speakers. But elsewhere, ethnic Germans in millions would be 'displaced' by restored 'free' governments and brutal mob action from areas where their families had lived for generations. Over most of Europe, the end of the war did not bring comfort and harmony. Starvation and new kinds of misery were more common.

OVERLEAF: **Before the Potsdam Conference, 17 July 1945, Berlin. British Chiefs of Staff inspect a naval guard of honour.**

This was taken at Berlin airport before the start of the conference. From left to right we see Field Marshal Sir Alan Brooke, Admiral Sir Andrew Cunningham and Air Marshal Sir Charles Portal. Berlin, which had fallen to the Soviet Red Army at the end of April, was to be divided into sections under the four main allies (France being included). Just outside the devastated city, the last of three meetings of Allied Heads of State occurred. (The previous ones had been at Teheran in 1943 and Yalta in February 1945.) But there were new faces. Harry S Truman had replaced the dead Roosevelt as US President. On 21 July, there was a review of British troops in the Tiergarten, Berlin. As Churchill drove up to the reviewing stand, British soldiers on the other side of the street cheered loudly. Churchill acknowledged what he thought was tribute to him by raising his hand with two fingers making his famous V-sign. But he dropped it as the soldiery, began to chant 'Attlee! Attlee! Attlee!' in honour of the figure seated in the next vehicle, a person whom Churchill had once described as 'a modest little man with plenty to be modest about'. Stalin watched in disbelief as Churchill, defeated in the British General Election according to results announced on 26 July, as a democrat, humbly accepted the decision of his people and went home. So did the unassuming Attlee, who had accompanied him as his deputy, but returned on 28 July as Prime Minister with his Labour Foreign Secretary, Ernest Bevin. The chief result of the conference was agreement on a call to Japan to surrender and on the terms on which that country would be occupied. Also, the post-war German-Polish frontier was de facto settled along the lines of the rivers Oder and Neisse. Poland was compensated for land within the country's pre-war frontiers, now devoured by the Soviet Union, with territory previously part of Germany. It was understood, though not unambiguously laid down, that Germans would be 'ethnically cleansed' from these areas.

The conference closed on 2 August. Four days later, President Truman announced that a US plane had dropped an 'atom bomb' on Hiroshima, Japan, on 5 August. For leaders and diplomats, the world would never be the same again.

FURTHER READING

Paul Addison, *The Road to 1945*, 1975

Paul Addison and Angus Calder (eds.),*Time to Kill: The Soldier's Experience of World War II in the West, 1939–1945*, 1997

Corelli Barnett, *Engage the Enemy More Closely: The Royal Navy in the Second World War,* 1991

Angus Calder, *The People's War: Britain 1939–1945*, 1969

Angus Calder, *The Myth of the Blitz,*1991

Angus Calder (ed.), *Wars*, 1999

Jeremy Crang, *The British Army and the People's War, 1939-1945*, 2000

ICB Dear (ed), *The Oxford Companion to the Second World War*, (new edition), 2001

Len Deighton, *Fighter;The True Story of the Battle of Britain*, 1979

Ian Hamilton (ed.), *The Poetry of War*, 1965

Samuel Hynes, *The Soldiers' Tale: Bearing Witness to Modern War*, 1998

Anne Powell (ed.), *Shadows of War: British Women's Poetry of the Second World War*, 1999

John Terraine, *The Right of the Line: The Royal Air Force in the European War 1939–1945*, 1985

Evelyn Waugh, *Sword of Honour*, 1965; edited A. Calder, 1999

Gerhard L Weinberg, *A World at Arms: A Global History of World War II*, 1994

ACKNOWLEDGEMENTS

All pictures reproduced from the Imperial War Museum archives:
pages: 6: tr 114, 8 & 82: tr 596, 15: col 300, 30: tr 2050, 32: tr 5052, 42: tr 2666, 44: tr 581, 48: tr 456, 50:tr 1420, 54: col 215, 60: tr 2389, 66: tr 139, 68: tr 111, 70: col 201, 74: tr 282, 76: tp 1, 78: tr 42, 80: tr 100, 82: tp 596, 84: tr 582, 88: tr 197, 90: tr 180, 94: tr 63, 96: tr60, 98: tr 60, 98: tr 48, 102: tr 210, 106: tr 2024, 110: tr 2024, 110: tr844, 112: tr 861, 116: tr 842, 118: tr 1228, 121: Monty, 124: tr 1093, 128: tr211, 130: tr2370, 134: tr 2828, 136: tr 1710, 138: tr 2851, 142: tr 2876, 145: col 194, 146: tr 2872, 150: tr 2910

Hamish Henderson: *Elegies for the Dead in Cyrenaica*: courtesy of Hamish Henderson
Keith Douglas: *Cairo Jag: Collected Poems*, Edited by John Waller and G.S. Fraser and J.C. Hall, published by Faber and Faber, 1966